WARRIORS & WORDS

WARRIORS & WORDS

Memoirs of Battles

Ricardo Mendoza

Columbus, Ohio

The views and opinions expressed in this book are solely those of the author and do not reflect the views or opinions of Gatekeeper Press. Gatekeeper Press is not to be held responsible for and expressly disclaims responsibility of the content herein.

Warriors & Words: Memoirs of Battles

Published by Gatekeeper Press
2167 Stringtown Rd, Suite 109
Columbus, OH 43123-2989
www.GatekeeperPress.com

Copyright © 2021 by Ricardo Mendoza
All rights reserved. Neither this book, nor any parts within it may be sold or reproduced in any form or by any electronic or mechanical means, including information storage and retrieval systems, without permission in writing from the author. The only exception is by a reviewer, who may quote short excerpts in a review.

The editorial work for this book is entirely the product of the author. Gatekeeper Press did not participate in and is not responsible for any aspect of these elements.

ISBN (paperback): 9781662919312

Foreword

Warfare has always existed and Plato instructs us that "only the dead have seen the end of war." With that context in mind, humans in all civilizations have attempted to sense and make sense of the necessity for and their experiences in combat. In the western tradition, ancient Greek plays, the awarding of honors and spoils to victors and participants, movies, songs, books, poems and whole cultural and national narratives have been used to do this. First Sergeant Mendoza, United States Marine Corps (Retired), is a true warrior, who has sensed combat up close and personal and has now extended the classical body of literature on warfare. He has compiled for the ages some of the thoughts and emotions of combat of our own lifetime. Though small in number, the messages are powerful for those of us who have experienced combat, who have made the profession of arms their vocation, or who wish to understand what the most interpersonal of endeavors has in store for its participants. The words in the pages ahead can be used to both sense and make sense of warfare. I have kept an unpublished draft version of this document on my desk side for some time and am excited to see it finally published for all to read and experience.

Col Gilbert D. Juarez
United States Marine Corps

Captain D. A. Zembiec inspired my journaling.
10 September 2001

This journal is designed for the owner to record their words in a small attempt to immortalize their memories.

10 September 2021

14 SEPT 41

TO SGT MENDOZA,

THANK YOU FOR MAKING MARINE RECON, AND THE CORPS, STRONGER.

PRESS THE ATTACK,

D.A. Bembiec
CAPT   USMC

The suffering amongst brothers is something few shall share.
Fort Story 2001

They will soon forget a coward's death.
They will always remember a warrior's life.
Annapolis 2007

They rest in peace for their sacrifice.
For their sacrifice the rest live in peace.
Arlington 2007

Pride is a counterfeit for courage.
All warriors will learn this lesson.
Quantico 2002

The sound of stallions storm through the black unknown.
Their feet thunder over the fields not yet sown.
Their steel will create fear in the enemies not yet shown.
Baptism by fire will be the newborn's broken home.
Man will continue to lose his life and soul in the black unknown.
Afghanistan 2012

Children's innocence, most at play.
Once a place of violence and fray.
Who could've imagined this joy and bliss.
After youth lost and families still miss.
Sons will soon take their father's place.
Surrendering to the flaws of the human race.
Normandy 2018

Warriors move forward into the Devil's Abyss.
The evil they pursue often follows them home.
Finding asylum in the dark corners of their soul.
                      Kandahar 2012

It is the teenager who shall take countless steps on distant lands who shapes the battlefield and politics of war.
Tikrit 2003

Warriors do not work under assurances.
We commit to the will of our tribe.
Helmand 2010

Do you surrender your principles to maintain your status?
or
Do you surrender your status to maintain your principles?
Diyala River 2003

Cold are the heavy stones of guilt.
Warm are the floating embers of forgiveness.
Tikrit 2003

Words can be the windows to your life.
Give those who love you a view into your soul.
Home 2019

Against a skilled insurgency
mastery of your heart is the greatest weapon.
Pakistan 2007

Man's journey through war is a cynical dance
>   between anger and kindness
>   lacking rhythm and balance.
>   Afghanistan 2012

When you end the illusion of control
you begin the clarity of thought.
Helmand 2010

Living with courage is pure freedom.
Without it you imprison yourself in fear.
Camp Pendleton 2003

If you have the audacity to fight your enemy on their terms,
surely you can love your soulmate on theirs.
Pakistan 2008

Love is the seed that inspires greatness.
Hate is the weed that strangles it.
Whittier 2017

Home is not where you rest your head.
Rather, it is where you rest your heart.
Los Angeles 2017

It makes no errors.
It has no strangers.
It will destroy darkness.
It is complete nakedness.
It is infinite humility.
It is universal reality.
It is love and grace.
It is a perfect place.
Iraq 2003

Peace resides where expectations and reality collide.
Whittier 2019

Acknowledgements

Thank you to my alma mater, Whittier College.

Words cannot express my gratitude towards my family and friends who endured my absence and awaited my return with open arms.

Dedicated to the junior enlisted, who rarely have a voice, and always endure the "lion's share" of combat.

My esteem and empathy is reserved for the small fraternity of warriors who carry with them the first hand experience of primordial intraspecies violence and fought until they succumbed to the internecine of warfare.

www.ingramcontent.com/pod-product-compliance
Lightning Source LLC
LaVergne TN
LVHW042003060526
838200LV00041B/1856